Dealing with Fe[el]ing...
Angry

Isabel Thomas

Illustrated by Clare Elsom

Raintree is an imprint of Capstone Global Library Limited, a company incorporated in England and Wales having its registered office at 7 Pilgrim Street, London, EC4V 6LB – Registered company number: 6695582

www.raintreepublishers.co.uk
myorders@raintreepublishers.co.uk

Text © Capstone Global Library Limited 2013
First published in hardback in 2013
Paperback edition first published in 2014
The moral rights of the proprietor have
been asserted.

Edited by Dan Nunn, Rebecca Rissman, and
  Catherine Veitch
Designed by Philippa Jenkins
Original illustrations © Clare Elsom
Illustrated by Clare Elsom
Production by Victoria Fitzgerald
Originated by Capstone Global Library Ltd
Printed and bound in China

ISBN 978 1 406 25037 4 (hardback)
16 15 14 13 12
10 9 8 7 6 5 4 3 2 1

ISBN 978 1 406 25047 3 (paperback)
17 16 15 14
10 9 8 7 6 5 4 3 2 1

British Library Cataloguing in Publication Data
Thomas, Isabel.
Angry. -- (Dealing with Feeling...)
152.4'7-dc23
A full catalogue record for this book is available from the British Library.

Contents

Some words are shown in bold, **like this.** Find out what they mean in the glossary on page 23.

What is anger?

happy

shy

caring

sad

Anger is a **feeling**. It is normal to have many kinds of feelings every day.

Everyone feels angry sometimes. We might feel angry when something hurts us, annoys us, or seems unfair.

How do we know when someone is angry?

Our faces and bodies can show other people how we are feeling. Also, we may show how we are feeling in the way that we behave.

Some people go quiet or cry when they are angry. Other people may shout, or try to hurt people or break things.

What does anger feel like?

Anger can make you feel hot and shaky inside. You might feel as if the anger is trapped inside your body, waiting to burst out.

It can be easy to get angry. It can
be harder to stop being angry.
Trying to hide angry **feelings** can
make you feel worse.

Is it okay to feel angry?

Two children at a time

When somebody else breaks the rules, it can make you lose your temper. Many people feel angry when something is unfair.

It is okay to feel angry, but it is not okay to hurt people. You need to find a safe way to let anger out.

11

How can I deal with anger?

Being told off for something that you did not do can make you feel angry. It is okay to feel angry, but it is not okay to shout at people or be rude.

The best way to deal with **feelings** is to talk about them. You could tell the person who made you angry how you feel.

What if I am too angry to talk?

When someone makes fun of you, it can make you feel cross. It is okay to feel angry, but it is not okay to **damage** other people's things.

Find a safe way to let your anger out. You could scribble on scrap paper or tear up old newspaper.

What are safe ways to let anger out?

It can be **frustrating** to not be the winner. It is okay to feel bad, but it is not okay to punch, kick, or throw things.

Exercise is a safe way to let anger out. You could go for a run or a walk, or jump up and down.

How can I help myself to calm down?

When something you have made gets broken, you might feel angry. It is okay to feel grumpy, but it is not okay to fight.

Calm down by walking away. Try taking ten deep breaths. You could drink a glass of water to cool yourself down.

How can I help someone else who is angry?

Everyone feels angry sometimes, even grown-ups. Sometimes angry people are not nice to other people, because they are feeling bad inside.

When they calm down, they might want to talk about how they feel. You can help by listening.

Make an anger toolbox

Write down some tips to help you deal with angry **feelings.**

Scribble on some paper, and then tear it up into tiny pieces.

Have a cool drink.

Take ten deep breaths.

Look at nice pictures or listen to music.

Take time out.

Talk to somebody that you trust about how you feel.

Draw a picture to show what made you angry.

Stamp your feet or run outside.

Don't be afraid to ask for help. Everyone needs help sometimes.

Glossary

damage do harm to something

feeling something that happens inside our minds. It can affect our bodies and the way we behave.

frustrating something that makes us feel upset or annoyed because we cannot change it

Find out more

Books

Everybody Feels: Angry, Jane Bingham (QED Publishing, 2006)

When Sophie Gets Angry – Really, Really Angry, Molly Bang (Scholastic, 2008)

Websites

bbc.co.uk/scotland/education/health/feelings

kidshealth.org/kid/feeling

pbskids.org/arthur/games/aboutface

Index